THE ROAD TO GLORY

A celebration of the achievements
of Britain's disabled athletes

Richard & Fiona Bailey

Quiller Press
London

First published 1996 by Quiller Press Ltd, 46 Lillie Road, London SW6 1TN.
ISBN 1899163 27 1

Book design by **Steve Gardiner and Debbie Downing**.
Photographic prints by **Richard Bailey**.
Photographic materials supplied by **Ilford**.
Printed by **Colorcraft Ltd. Hong Kong.**

THE ROAD TO GLORY

Photographs by **Richard & Fiona Bailey**

FOREWORD

It is with great pride that Sunrise Medical, whose mobility products including 'Quickie' and 'Shadow' have become totally synonymous with sports equipment, has chosen to make a substantial commitment to the 1996 Paralympic Games as a major, official sponsor. **From the very first** Paralympics in 1960 when Sir Ludwig Guttmann, a neurosurgeon at Stoke Mandeville, conceived of the idea as being beneficial for rehabilitation for his patients with spinal injuries, the ideals have remained true. The Games have been run in a four year cycle, and the sphere of disability sport has increased immeasurably not only in terms of participation, awareness and support, but also reward. **The original base of 400 competitors** from 23 countries in 1960 grew to an impressive 3,500 competitors from 82 countries at the Barcelona Games in '92, where the British team achieved a laudable 40 Gold Medals, 47 Silver and 41 Bronze. **This phenomenal growth** has also seen the advent of new technology in mobility sports equipment at Sunrise, where an outstanding R&D team has honed and refined our products to the point where today they are a virtual extension of the athlete's body, and lead to optimum performance. **But perhaps it is still** the original vision of Sir Ludwig Guttmann which so succinctly captures the essence of the Paralympics, and reflects the constant mission of Sunrise as we strive to provide freedom, independence and empowerment through innovative design. He said: "By restoring activity of mind and body, by instilling self respect, self discipline, a competitive spirit and comradeship - sport develops mental attitudes that are essential for social integration." **The aim of our sponsorship** of the Paralympics is to involve the entire country and beyond in support of our world-class athletes, and Sunrise is again proud to join forces with Richard and Fiona Bailey on an initiative which will undoubtedly help to fulfil this aim. **'The Road to Glory'** will drive our athletes forward on their journey to Atlanta where they will represent Great Britain, and we wish them every success in their endeavours.

Ian Burrows
Managing Director, Sunrise Medical Ltd.

Official Sponsor • 1996 Paralympics

Sunrise Medical Ltd is a major sponsor of the 1996 Atlanta Paralympics

Tanni Grey won four gold medals at the Barcelona Paralympics in 1992; setting two world records and two Paralympic records in her wheelchair track races. Combining her post-graduate studies with training she has gone on to dominate her events, winning four gold medals at the World Championships in Berlin 1994 and the London Marathon of the same year.

The Paralympic Games is the biggest sporting event for disabled athletes in the world. But what do they actually mean to the public at large? The generic meaning and the original idea behind the Paralympics was simply that they run in parallel to the Olympic Games. In early years - dating back to the 1960s in a time when they were still titled 'Games for the Disabled' - the concept was slightly more vague, merely meaning a Games that would be run every four years, with the 'feeling' of the Olympic spirit embodied into disabled sport.

The meaning of the Paralympic Games to any athlete is altogether more powerful and dynamic. For any of the 250 athletes that make up the British Team, competing in 19 summer sports, the Paralympic Games is the highest level of competition that they can aspire to compete at. Before it is even possible to represent the British Team, there are hurdles to overcome. For many, making the team is the true achievement, as the selection process alone can be arduous. Distances have to be reached, time standards met, and all with one goal - the attainment of 'elite' performance. **The public** see the games as the opening ceremony and the competition. They rarely see the years of effort, dedication, sometimes hardship, commitment from supporters and loved ones, and also the pain and joy, the ups and downs, the constant setting and resetting of goals. There is little to compare to the pressure and strain that the athletes feel as this is the final chance to compare their performances against the best in the world.

The opening ceremony of the Games is an extremely special time for all athletes - it is an occasion filled with excitement, and some trepidation, because it signifies that everything is starting. Nothing compares to the magic of being there, proudly wearing the British kit waiting to enter the packed stadium. There are probably few people who could put in to words the emotion and feeling that is felt when this happens. This point also finally concurs that there is very little that can now be done to improve the performance. ***This is it!!*** The Games are the only thing that matters. **At the Games,** if the athlete's performance is good - either in terms of winning medals or breaking a personal goal - then it can provide a tremendous high. It is everything that you dreamt it could be - a special moment that will be treasured for life. Few are lucky enough to experience the elation and pride when on the medal podium with the Union Jack blowing in the wind, and the National Anthem boldly playing through the stadium. **This book** provides a different insight in to the athletes that represent Great Britain in Atlanta in1996. Each photograph shows a human perspective - the tangible side of what each athlete does, getting closer to the real person than will be possible during the Paralympic Games. The Paralympics is about winning and losing, ability, performance, and representing Britain with a pride in sporting achievement. There is no doubt that each athlete will do their best to fulfil the hopes of everyone around them to make it the best Games ever.

Tanni Grey MBE

C O N T E N T S

INTRODUCTION

The modern day Paralympic Games were born from the vision of Sir Ludwig Guttmann, a neurosurgeon at Stoke Mandeville Hospital in Aylesbury, England. **1n 1944**, a spinal injuries centre was set up at Stoke Mandeville hospital, under the direction of Sir Ludwig, and from the start sporting activities were introduced as part of the treatment and became integral to the rehabilitation programme at the unit. **The first sports** to be introduced were Archery and wheelchair Polo. From this it wasn't long before competition began to take place and the first was between a team of ex-service patients from the Star and Garter home, Richmond, and a team of servicemen and women from Stoke Mandeville Hospital. **Sir Ludwig** opened these first Stoke Mandeville games on 28th July 1948. This date was chosen as it coincided with King George VI opening of the Olympic Games in London and was symbolic in its deliberate attempt to connect the Olympics and Paralympics. **In 1952** a team of paraplegic war veterans from Holland crossed the channel to take part in the games. Thus, Great Britain and the Netherlands had the honour to become the co-founders of the International Stoke Mandeville Games for the Paralysed, which has since embraced over 70 countries. **The first official** Paralympic games were held in Rome in 1960, just a few weeks after the Olympics, where four hundred athletes from 23 countries joined together, to show the world that the Paralympic Movement had been created. **Sir Ludwig**, the driving force behind these games, was told, in a private audience with Pope John XXIII, "You are the Coubertin of the Paralysed!" **Since then**, the two events have held a 'parallel' existence being held, where possible, in the same city. The Rome Paralympics were followed by Tokyo 1964, Israel 1968, Heidelberg 1972, Toronto 1976, Arnhem 1980, Stoke Mandeville and New York 1984, Seoul 1988 and Barcelona 1992.

In the first years, only wheelchair athletes competed, but, as the Paralympic Movement grew, other classes of athletes began to participate. In 1976 at the Toronto Games, in addition to the spinal cord injured, it was possible to include sections for amputees and visually impaired. This was a great step forward in spreading the International sports movement of the disabled. The Paralympics has now encompassed all types of disabilities under the four International Federations responsible for athletes with a certain type of disability: paraplegics and tetraplegics; the blind and visually impaired; people with cerebral palsy, and amputees; and Les Autres (people with polio sequela, muscular dystrophy etc). **Participants in** the Paralympic Games are the best athletes from these four federations and, as such, the Paralympic Games are the zenith of competition for elite athletes with physical disabilities and only those athletes who have met strict qualifying standards are selected to represent his or her national team. **In those early days** Sir Ludwig could have only dreamt of how the sports movement for the paralysed could have developed into the hugely successful Games of the modern day we see now. But, his ideal of the games *embodying friendship, unity and sportsmanship*, resisting racial, religious and political barriers, will be evident at the Xth paralympiad, in Atlanta 1996, as it has been since those first games in 1948.

sport is for everyone
enjoy

1

Archery has always been a leading sport in the world of disabled athletes, since its inclusion in the Stoke Mandeville games of 1948. Balance, accuracy and intense concentration are all essential for both the standing and wheelchair competitors in this event. **As in the Olympic games** the event programmed is the Olympic FITA round, with both individual and team events. **Joan Cooper** and Val Williamson are veterans of the archery scene, having won medals in many International competitions. Andy Bayliss and Sandy Gregory in the wheelchair competition will be looking to compound their European Golds and Kathy Smith in the women's standing event is likely to be on the medal table.

ARCHERY

It feels **exhilirating** to **win**, not only for myself but for the **team** and **country**

Above: **Val Williamson**
Opposite: **Sandy Gregory**

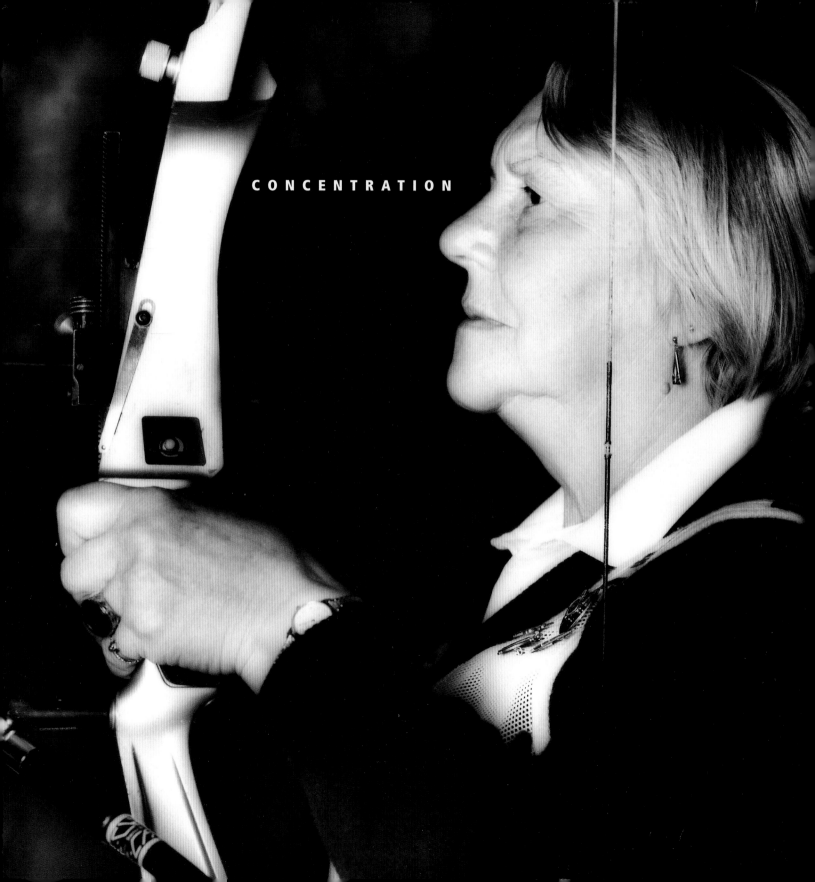

CONCENTRATION

Above: **John Mansell**
Opposite: **Joan Cooper**

You have to **prepare** your **mind** as
well as your **body**

Andy Bayliss

2

Athletics, with the events of track, throwing and jumping, pentathlon and the marathon, is the most widely watched of all the Paralympic competitions. Athletes from all the four federations take part; wheelchair athletes, blind athletes, amputees, and athletes with cerebral palsy - though not all compete in all the disciplines.

ATHLETICS

You **always** want to do well, but **especially**
when wearing a **Great Britain jersey**

Above and left: The 1995 **International**
Stoke Mandeville Games

Winning is my **inspiration**

Tanni Grey

Above: **Tanni Grey**
Left: **Chris Hallam**

Above: **Richard Powell**

With the crowd roaring their support and encouragement it is not surprising that athletes in these events produce some extraordinary results. In 1992, using two modern leg prosthesis, the U.S. athlete Tony Volpentest ran the TS2 category 100m in 11.63 seconds, only 1.77 seconds slower than Carl Lewis's record of 9.86. The one-armed Nigerian Ajibola Adeoye came within .86 of a second from Lewis's record when he recorded a time of 10.72 in the 100m. **Sebastian Coe's** 800m Olympic record of 1:41:71 lies next to Scot Hollonbeck's wheelchair Paralympic record of 1:40:63; and Marla Runyan, the visually impaired U.S. athlete, ran a 200m Paralympic record of 25.31 compared to Florence Griffith Joyners 21.34. **Wheelchair** marathoners regularly complete marathons in 90 minutes, averaging three-and-a-half minutes per mile over the full 26 mile course. **In the British** squad we already have some outstanding medal winners. The politics student from Cardiff, Tanni Grey MBE, is perhaps our most outstanding wheelchair athlete. In Barcelona 1992 she picked up four gold medals, setting two world records and two Paralympic records and since that triumph she has gone on to win the London Marathon as well as four world championship gold medals in 1994. **Nigel Coultas** has consistently been one of the world's top sprinters in his category over the last eight years. In Seoul 1988 he won three gold medals and in Barcelona he picked up three silver medals, two of them behind the awesome Ajibola Adeoye of Nigeria.

Top left: **Jack McKenna**
Top right: **John Harris**
Bottom left: **Rachel Potter**
Bottom right: **Rose Hill**

My aim for **Atlanta**
is to break the **world record**
I hold at 400m and to win
gold at 200m

Esther Cruice

Of the partially sighted competitors, Noel Thatcher from Harrow intends to emulate Emil Zapotek who won three gold medals in 1952 at 5,000m, 10,000m and the marathon. After winning gold in the 5,000m and 10,000m so often Noel believes he has the mental toughness and dedication to equal that feat. Bob Matthews, Tracey Hinton and Sharon Bolton will also be looking to add more medals to their collection in the track events. **The team** from cerebral palsy sport will be looking to surpass their medal achievements at the 1994 world championships in Berlin. Paul Williams will be looking to hold onto his world record in the Javelin, as will John Nethercott in the 1500m. **Esther Cruice**, Caroline Innes, Gordon Robertson and Kenny Churchill will all be confident in capturing gold after their successes in Berlin. **Apart from** Tanni Grey we can look to Jim Richardson, Andi Hodge, Rachel Potter, Rose Hill, Tracey Lewis and Sally Reddin among others to be on the medal podium for their wheelchair events. **The potential** performance of these young athletes at Atlanta and even in Sydney for the 2000 games can give us enormous optimism that the Union Jack will be flying high for a long time. **In the beginning** of sport for the disabled, athletes were expected to compete in the standard issue wheelchair and in those early days the wooden upholstered model was more of a hindrance than a help. **Over the years** wheelchair design changed and the heavy steel chair, although offering greater individual mobiltiy, was light years away from being an ideal sports chair. **In the 1980's** the athletes' demands for lightweight highly manoueverable sports chairs for racing and basketball in particular, led to experiments in design using light alloys. The wheelchair revolution has now advanced in such a way that the wheelchair has become specific and tailored to the individuals' size and requirements.

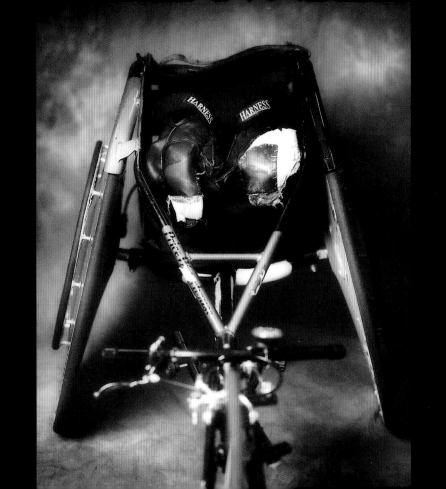

The old attitude of ***it's not the winning that counts, but the taking part*** means nothing to me. Just watch and listen to the Americans who say ***no-one remembers who was second***. So that's what I have in my head and it counts double when I am **competing** for Great Britain.

Jim Richardson

Right: **Paul Williams**
Left: **Jim Richardson**

Top left: **Douglas Greer**
Top right: **Rob Latham**
Bottom left: **Ivan Newman**
Bottom right: **Kenny Churchill**
Opposite: **Bob Mathews (right), Gary Heath (left)**

3

Wheelchair Basketball is one of the oldest established of the wheelchair sports; with its roots going back to the late 1940's/50's it was part of the first Paralympic games. Initially a rehabilitation and recreational activity for spinal cord injured patients, it quickly developed into a competition sport and today the National Wheelchair Basketball League of Great Britain consists of 44 teams playing in three divisions.

BASKETBALL

POSITIV

Encompassing a wide range of disabilities, including paraplegics, spina bifidas, amputees, brittle bones, cerebral palsy and multiple sclerosis, a classification system ensures that the more severely disabled athletes are not left out of the game. **All disabled** persons have a points value on court and the more severely disabled a player is the less points they are given. For instance, a single leg amputee could be a 4 or 4.5 point player, whereas a high lesion paraplegic could be a 1 point player. A team must put out on court five players whose total points must not exceed 14. **Matches last** 40 minutes real time and follow FIBA rules. The court and basket height are the same as in Olympic Basketball, though the three second limit inside the zone is extended to five seconds. **In winning the** 1995 European Basketball Championship, the men's team took the first major title for a British team in the sport since the early 1970's. This win followed up their silver the year before and shows not only the tremendous improvements made in the last decade, but explains why they are **main** contenders for Paralympic gold in Atlanta.

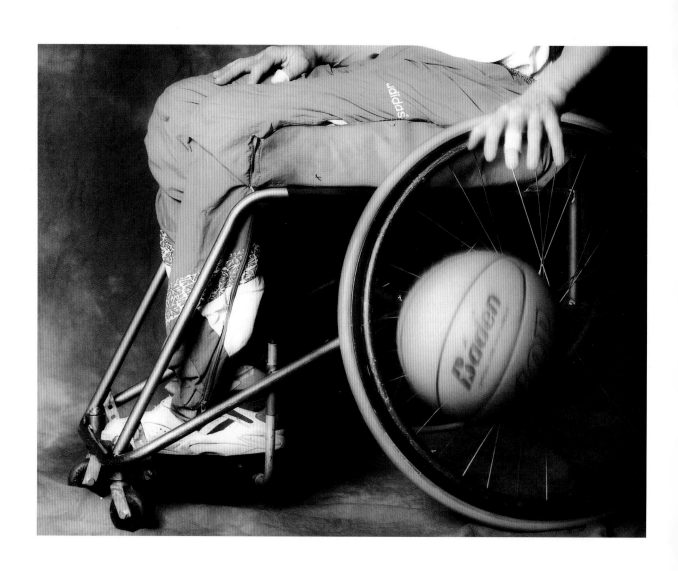

To **win** you need a combination

of **pure dedication**, and the

commitment to being part

of the team

Joe Jayaratne

TEAMWORK

You have to develop **mental toughness** to block out your surroundings when you are **competing**

4

CYCLING

Cycling is a relative newcomer to the competitions involved in the Paralympic games. Competition rules are the same as those laid down by the International Amateur Cycling Federation, with certain modifications, as regards the cycles themselves, safety measures and the classification of cyclists. **The participants** are divided into three groups according to disability: cerebral palsy, visual impairment and impaired mobility, and compete in road racing and time trials. **Current double world champion, Thomas Evans**, added two more golds to his collection, in the cerebral palsy 5,000m and 21km road race at the European championships, held in Germany 1995. Looking forward to Atlanta, Thomas has included in his training schedule a unique way of acclimatising to the intense heat and humidity he will face there. Central heating on full blast, pans of boiling water on the stove, kitchen door closed and hours spent on the training bike!. **Visually impaired Robert Allen**, a relative newcomer to the sport, along with his pilot Kathryn Miles, are likely candidates to follow up their European championship gold in the mixed tandem 1,000m sprint.

DEDICATION

Left: **Alan Davy**
Right: **Clive Wilsher**
Opposite page: **Robert Allen and Kath Miles**

When I hear commentators say it is lovely that **disabled people**
can take part in sport, and that they do it **for fun**, I think about
all the times I get **up at 5am** ride up a hill for five miles
non stop and almost collapse at the top from exhaustion.
The word fun is not on my mind, **winning is!**

Robert Allen

The number one thing is **to win,** and when you do the feeling of **pride** is immense and you think **I've done it for my country**

Thomas Evans

Left: **Thomas Evans**

5

The first riding for the disabled World Championships were in Sweden in 1987, where Great Britain picked up two gold medals. Since then it has been held in Denmark in 1991 and England in 1995. **Although** people with disabilities have been riding throughout the century, the Riding for the Disabled Assocoation of Great Britain was officially formed in 1969. There are now 700 groups with over 26,000 adult and children riders. **Competitors** are classified into four groups according to their disability and ride dressage tests specially written by IPEC, on either 'borrowed' or 'own nation' horses. Riders on their own horses are judged in a separate class. **The set tests** for Grades I and II consist of walk and trot only. Grade III and IV include canter, and Grade IV encompasses lateral movements in which the horse advances sideways and forward at the same time. **These tests** must be performed in a specific sequence of movements and in precise patterns, governed by markers around the arena.

EQUESTRIAN

Opposite: **Liz Stone**
Below top: **Pat Straughan**
Bottom: **Sharon Blunden**

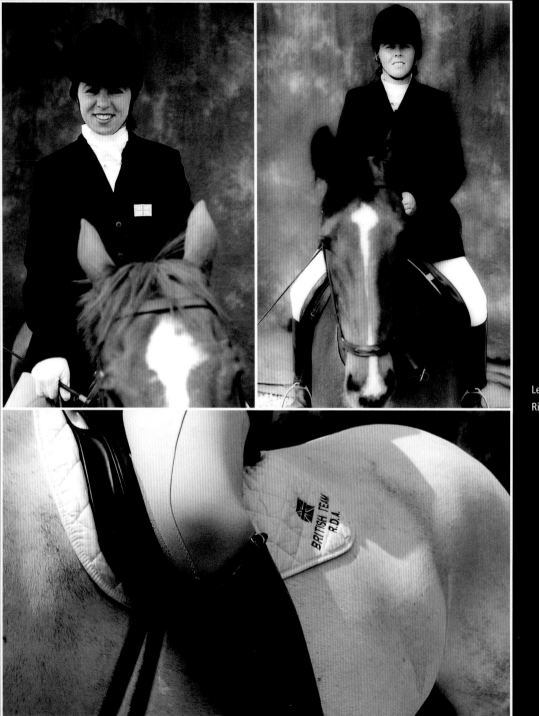

Left: **Susan Poulton**
Right: **Anne Dunham**

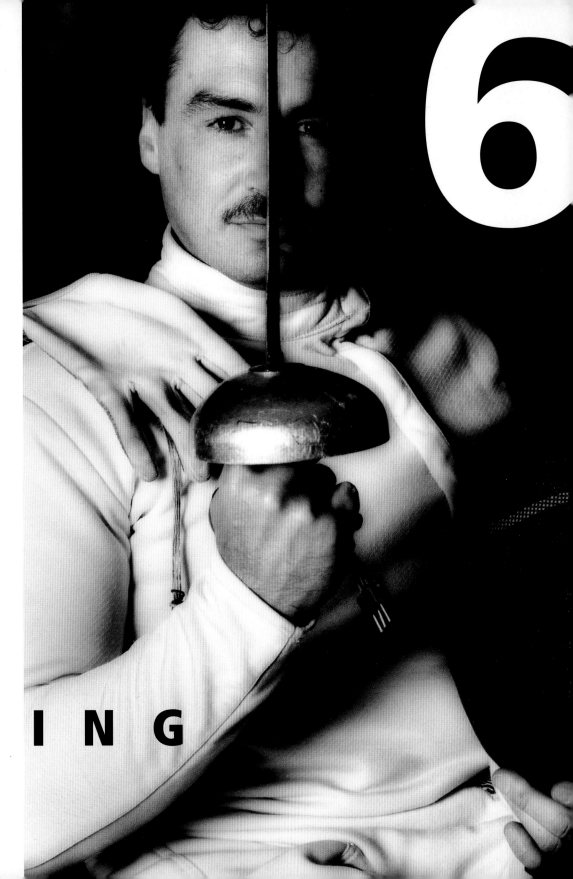

6

FENCING

Fencing in wheelchairs for the disabled was first introduced by Sir Ludwig Guttmann in 1954/55 and has formed part of the Paralympic programme since the first games in Rome 1960. **The sport** features wheelchair athletes, amputees and athletes with cerebral palsy. The most striking characteristic of this sport is that competitors are seated in wheelchairs, which are fastened to the floor by guides which do not impede body movement. **There is just one** set of International rules which differ from those of traditional fencing, these are regarding the distance between competitors and the fact that in the sabre competition the valid target is formed by the entire upper section of the body. **Competitors face each other** in their wheelchairs with 'plastrons' covering the lower part of the body, which is not a valid hit zone. The events are the Foil discipline, where the target area is the trunk only; the Epée discipline where the target area is anywhere above the waist, and the Sabre. The aim is to secure points by penetrating your opponents defence and touching them on the specified areas of the body, with the first person to score five points the winner. **Caz Walton** has been top of her sport for 20 years, having competed in five Paralympic games. Starting in 1972 at Heidelberg, Germany, she won a gold in the foil event, another gold in Seoul 1988 and she returned with gold, silver and bronze from the world games in 1990. Other names to look out for on the medal list at Atlanta are Kevin Davies and Suzannah Rockett.

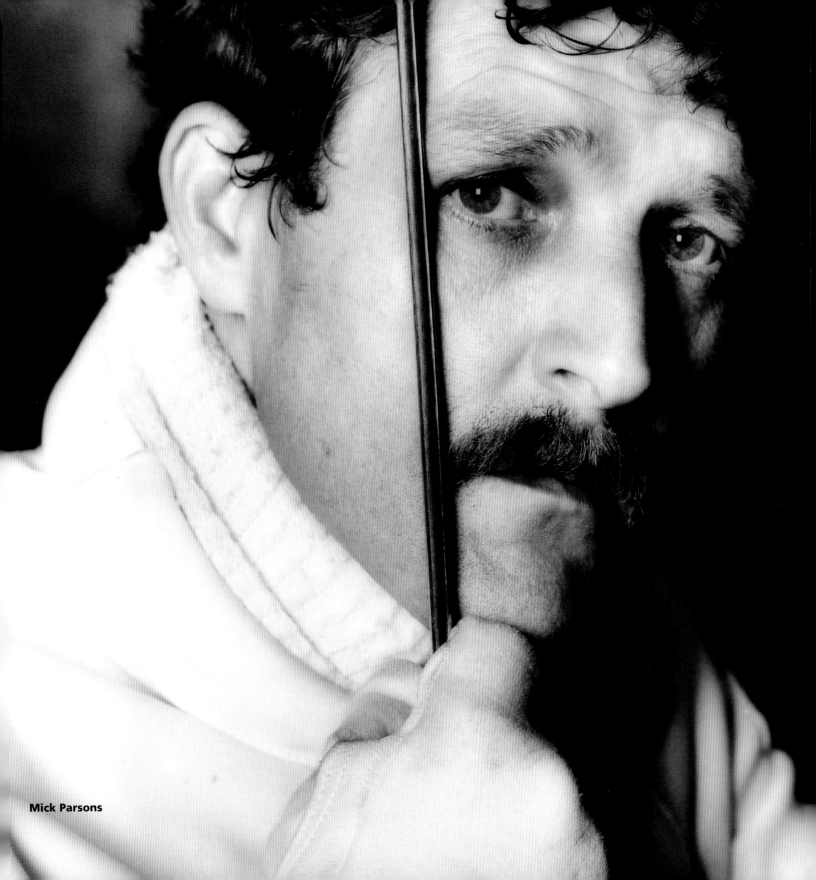

Mick Parsons

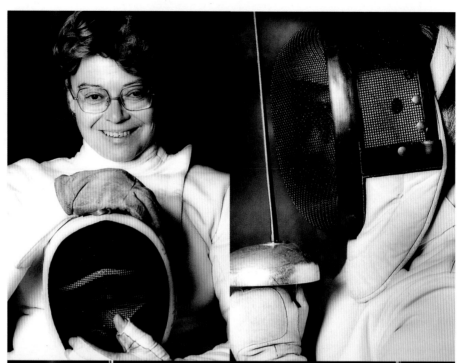

Top left: **Caz Walton**
Top right: **Keith Mitton**
Bottom left: **Keith Mitton**
Bottom right: **Suzannah Rockett**
Opposite: **Jason Byerley**

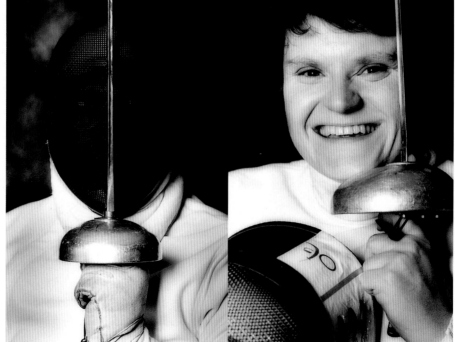

You put your **career** on hold and hope that you can **justify**

all the help people have given and the **commitment** that you

have put in, not only the **time and effort**, but the

7

Seven-a-side Soccer is the variant of football, played at the Paralympic games, by athletes with varying degrees of cerebral palsy. The rules follow those of FIFA, with a number of modifications to accomodate the disabilities of the players. **For example**, throw-ins can be taken using one arm only and not neccesarily go over shoulder height; up to three substitutes may be made during the match and there is no off-side law. Matches are divided into halves of 20 minutes each, with 10 minutes for half time. **At the Barcelona games** the Dutch started off as hot favourites and proved everyone right by lifting the trophy, after beating Portugal in the final. The British team, beaten into fourth place by the Irish in Barcelona, were unfortunately knocked out in the qualifying rounds and will not be making the trip to Atlanta.

F O O

ALL

8

lball is a sport played by the blind and visually impaired, which has its origins in Germany
Austria from the middle part of this century. It is played on a court with a goal at each
, which occupies the entire width of the court, 9m, and is 1.3m high. There are three players
ach side who try to score by throwing the ball into the opposition's goalmouth.

GOALBALL

As the players all wear goggles, which are checked to ensure no vision is possible, goalball can be played by disabled athletes with varying degrees of vision. The court is divided into three areas, defence, throwing and neutral and all the lines are marked out on the court using rough adhesive tape to help the players take up their positions. **The ball contains** bells to orient the players and to indicate the direction it is taking, which means that during play spectators must maintain complete silence so that the players can concentrate and follow the ball. **A good defence** will try to cover as much space as possible and once they have sensed the direction of the ball they must dive to stop it from entering their goalmouth. A good attack is trying to keep the ball as still as possible before throwing it, so that your opponent will be unaware from which direction it is coming.

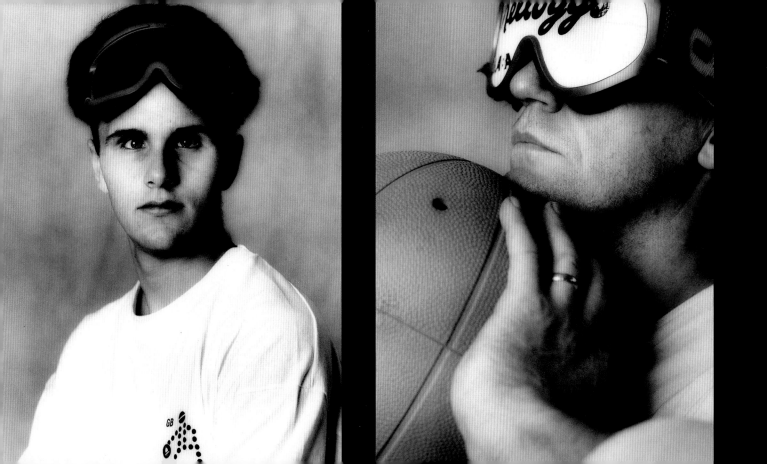

COMMITM

The whole ethos of the **Olympic dream** is my **inspiration** and everything that that ideal holds is a real **driving force**

Tony Reddish

N T

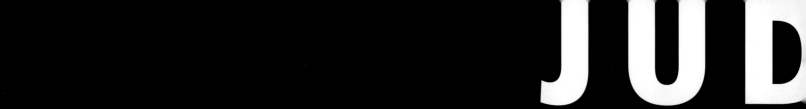

9

…do is practised** by blind and visually impaired competitors and follows the rules set by the …ernational Judo Federation, with certain modifications. **The requirements** of the sport …olving an acute sense of touch and ability and instinct in running the fine line between balance …d imbalance makes Judo an ideal sport for those persons with certain disabilities. **The danger …ne**, or red zone, of the 'Tatami' can be made out by touch, and the competitors are helped …o initial contact for the bout by the referee. Competition is divided into seven weight categories …d has been a Paralympic sport since the VIII Games in Seoul. **The Rochdale born** Judoka, …mon Jackson** (pictured left), is the current world and European champion. Since winning the …d medal in the 60kg category at the Seoul games he has had an unbeaten 65 straight …ernational winning streak, including the gold medal in the 70kg category at the Barcelona games.

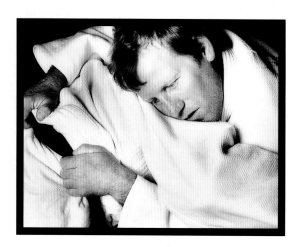

Above: **Mick Murch**
Right: **Ian Rose**

Above left: **Phil Hall**
Above right: **Terry Powell**

There is **only one thing** that is going through my mind when I compete and that is **I am going to win**

Ian Rose

P O W E

If you don't have the **commitment** to

work hard you won't **succeed**

10

Weightlifting and Powerlifting have both been Paralympic sports since the II Games in Tokyo, 1964, and are, in their basic features and rules, the same as the Olympic Games. The competition differs in that the only event is the bench press. **At Atlanta** for the first time there will only be the Powerlifting event. This is where lying on a bench the competitor takes the bar at arms length, brings the weight down to his/her chest, pauses, then presses back to arms length.

IFTING

It is a sport open to wheelchair athletes, amputees and competitors with cerebral palsy and is structured according to the classic body weight categories. **In the 100kg** and the **48kg** categories we have winners in the shape of Nicky Slater and Anthony Peddle respectively. Both won medals in their classes at Barcelona and at the European championships in France, 1995. Nicky put in a massive lift of 200kg to win gold. Anthony lifted over three times his body weight to win silver, whilst Russell Wiley and Alan Cullen are others to look out for.

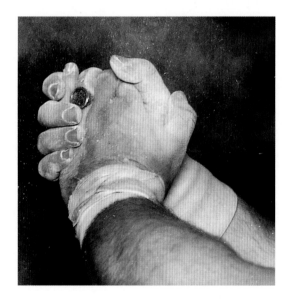

Left: **Nicky Slater**

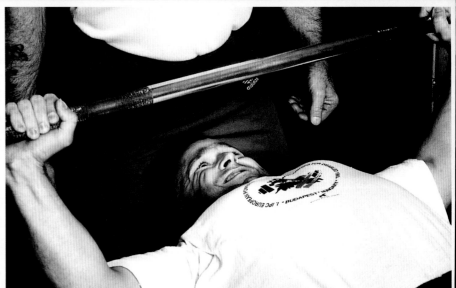

Above: **Russell Wiley**
Opposite: **Anthony Peddle**

The human **potential** to overcome any **adversity**, especially in the sporting arena, never ceases to **amaze** me, and this is my **inspiration**

In the Sailing competition Great Britain are represented by World and European champions, Terry Downs, Kevin Curtis and Andy Cassel. In Rutland, England, Terry and Andy were in the team that won the 1994 World Championships sailing a 'squib' and helping Great Britain to take the team trophy as well. In September of 1995, with Kevin on board they went on to win the first ever European Championships held in Mar-Menor Murcia, Spain; this time in a 'Randsmeer' boat. **The Sailing competition** is for all disability classes and for men and women - competing in 3 person team events - and consists of a series of races around courses set by the organising committee. In Atlanta the course will be set by the Olympic committee and the duration of the race should be approximately 1-1½ hours for the first boat to cross the finish line.

11

SAILING

securicor
security services

The amount of races held depends on the days of competition, though in Atlanta there will be 7 races. The low scoring system will be used, such that the winner of each race is awarded zero points and, when all the races have been completed, the team with the lowest score has won. **In Atlanta** competitors will sail in provided 'sonar' class yachts - these are 3 person keel boats with a length of about 23 feet and a sail area of 22.5 square metres.

Top: **Kevin Curtis**
Bottom: **Andy Cassel**
Previous page: **Tony Downs**

The **Shooting competition** is divided into rifle and pistol events in the air gun and .22 calibre categories. The competition is open to amputees, wheelchair athletes and competitors with cerebral palsy; with men's, women's and mixed events on the programme. **The rules** are the same as those of the International Shooting Union, with a number of modifications to accomodate the disabilities of those taking part. **The use of** electronic targets and automatic scoreboards was a major technological innovation at the Barcelona games.

12

SHOOTING

Isobel Newstead is another legend in the world
of Paralympic sport. In Seoul she competed in the sports
of wheelchair shooting (air pistol), shot, javelin, discus
and swimming. She came home with a gold in the discus,
silver in the shot and bronze in both air pistol and javelin!

Multi medallist Deanna Coates will be making her fourth consecutive Paralympic games when she competes in Atlanta. Deanna was in the medal table in 1984 with two silvers and a bronze, following that with a gold in Seoul and another gold in Barcelona. The wheelchair shooter also won the British Air Rifle Championship for women in 1989, in competition with able-bodied shooters.

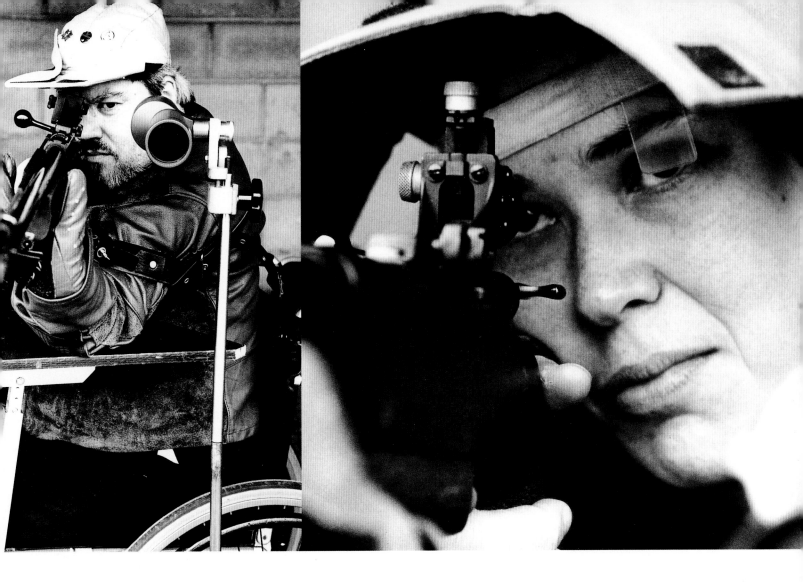

Above right: **Karen Butler**

Above left: **Keith Morris**

You have to have **tunnel vision**,

just see the gun sight and **target**

and **nothing else matters**

Above and right: **Robert Cooper**

Top: **Claire Hirst**
Bottom: **Paul Pantzer**

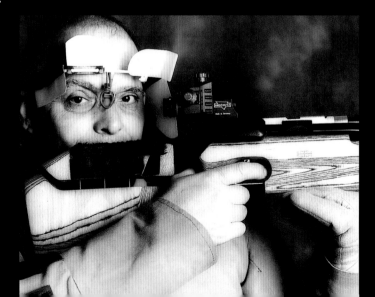

you need a moment of **complete concentration**

60 times over a period of **2 hours**

Everything that you have worked towards is condensed into a

split second when you have **won** and all the hard work and early

mornings were worth it and you know that you **deserve it**

Chris Holmes

13 SWIMMING

Chris Holmes MBE

Swimming has been a Paralympic sport since the first games in Rome, 1960. It has its origins in physiotherapy and rehabilitation, but soon became one of the most widely competed, and spectated, of all the Paralympic sports. **Swimmers** with all types of disability take part, competing by gender and in two groups: one for the blind and visually impaired and the second for swimmers with mobility impairments, including amputees and wheelchair athletes. **The events** are limited to the four official Olympic styles; Back-stroke, breast-stroke, freestyle and butterfly. According to the disability of the competitor, he or she may start in the water or from the edge of the pool and blind swimmers are warned when approaching the end of the pool by a volunteer tapping them with a 'bonker'. **Britain's swimmers** have always been high in the medal table since the sport's inception and now has many leading lights in the world of disabled sport. **Leading the way** is Chris Holmes MBE. The partially sighted politics student picked up a magnificent six gold medals and three world records at the Barcelona games, ensuring him a permanent place in Britain's Paralympic history books. **Peter Hull** MBE, one of Great Britain's seasoned internationals, won three gold medals, all in world record times, at the Barcelona Paralympiad and is proof of the quality of competition set by athletes with severe disability.

Other multi-medallists include Jeanette Esling, Margaret McEleny, Janice Burton, Traci Wiscombe, Melanie Easter, Sarah Bailey, Jane Stidever, Jim Anderson and Kenny Cairns. **Meanwhile** young newcomers such as Emily Jennings and Jody Cundy, who have been picking up golds in the World and Europeans are likely to make waves in Atlanta.

Right: **Jody Cundy**
Opposite page: **Emily Jennings**

You have to be **totally commited** to the **swim**

Chris Holmes

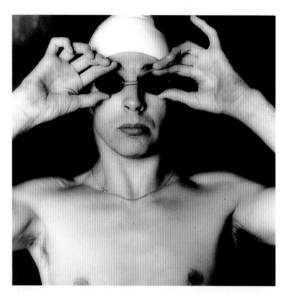

Top left: **Margaret McEleny**
Top right: **Kenny Cairns**
Bottom left: **Jim Anderson**
Bottom right: **Janice Burton**
Opposite page: **Paul Noble**

TABLE TENNIS

14

When you look around and see who you are **competing** against you feel an **incredible buzz** because it makes you realise you have reached the **highest level**

Neil Robinson

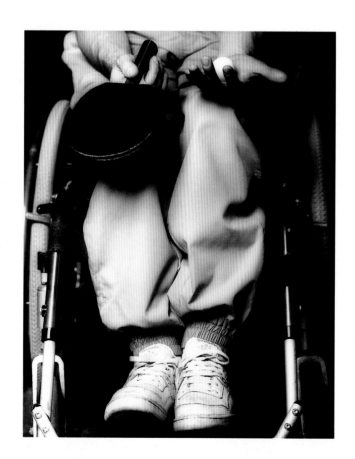

Table-tennis, a Paralympic sport since Rome 1960, involves both wheelchair and standing events. Both events follow the rules of the International Table-tennis Federation, with some small technical variations introduced for the wheelchair competition. **For example**, at service the ball must clear the end of the table, not the sides, and players may grip the table in order to retain their balance as long as the table is not moved. **Currently ranked** world number one, Neil Robinson from Bridgend, has been winning medals since his first international competition in 1981. In Barcelona he picked up a gold for the team event and a silver for the men's singles and during the World Games of 1993 he came away with two golds for the team event and men's singles.

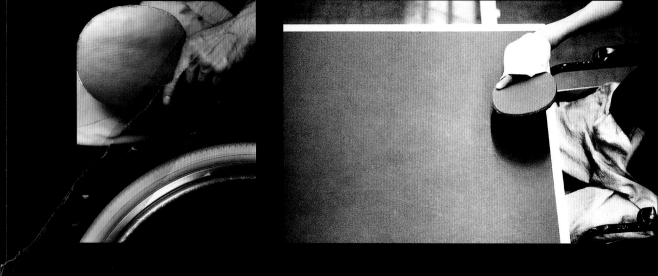

TENNIS
15

Simon Hatt

Brad Parks and Jeff Minnebraker, two disabled athletes from America, pioneered this new sport by giving a series of exhibitions of wheelchair Tennis to the disabled in 1976. Since that time wheelchair Tennis has been one of the fastest growing of all the wheelchair sports with over 6,000 people participating worldwide and tournaments being held in the United States, Europe and Asia. **In Britain**, tennis pro Brian Locke helped pioneer the development of this new sport after seeing it being played in Coventry in 1983. By 1985 Brian and others had formed the British Wheelchair Tennis Association. **In 1988** wheelchair Tennis was accepted as a demonstration sport at the Paralympics in Seoul, meaning that it would be accepted as a recognised sport for the Barcelona Games in 1992. **Wheelchair Tennis** is played according to the rules of tennis with one major exception, the players can let the ball bounce twice before playing it. **Wheelchair Tennis** is also unique in that, unlike other wheelchair sports where you are classified according to your level of disability, wheelchair tennis players are grouped according to their ability as a tennis player.

Left: **Kimberley Dell**
Opposite : **Andrea**
Broadway-Parkinson

110

Self-belief is the key, you have to know that you can beat anyone

and when you win your **aspirations** automatically go up, so that you

are constantly setting yourself new goals and knocking down barriers -

that is what makes people excel

Andrea Broadway-Parkinson

THE ATHLETES

THE ATHLETES

MEDAL TABLES

The 1992 Barcelona Paralympic Games medal table (top 5)

Nation	Gold	Silver	Bronze
USA	76	52	48
Germany	61	50	60
Britain	40	47	41
France	36	36	33
Spain	34	31	42

Britain's 1992 Barcelona Paralympic Games medal table by sport

Sport	total	gold	silver	bronze
Swimming	64	22	25	17
Athletics	51	15	20	16
table-tennis	4	1	1	2
shooting	4	1	0	3
judo	2	1	0	1
powerlifting	1	0	0	1
fencing	1	0	0	1
weight lifting	1	0	0	1

Britain's top medalists from the 1992 Barcelona Paralympic Games

Athlete	Gold	Silver	Bronze
Chris Holmes (swimming)	6	1	0
Tanni Grey (Athletics)	4	2	0
Janice Burton (swimming)	3	4	0
Peter Hull (swimming)	3	0	0
Sarah Bailey (swimming)	2	3	1
David Moreton (swimming)	2	0	1

The 1988 Seoul Paralympic Games medal table (top 5)

Nation	Gold	Silver	Bronze
USA	92	91	85
Germany	77	64	48
Great Britain	62	66	51
Canada	54	42	57
France	45	48	49

PARTICIPANTS

Number of participants at all paralympic games (growth of the games since its inception)

Year	Venue	Number of athletes and other participants	Delegations
1960	I Rome	400	23
1964	II Tokyo	390	22
1968	III Tel Aviv	1,100	29
1972	IV Heidelberg	1,400	44
1976	V Toronto	2,700	42
1980	VI Arnhem	2,560	42
1984	VII New York	1,700	41
1984	Stoke Mandeville	2,300	45
1988	VIII Seoul	4,200	62
1992	IX Barcelona	4,158	82

THE BRITISH PARALYMPIC ASSOCIATION (BPA)

The BPA was formed in 1989 with a membership made up of the disability group governing bodies with international sporting responsibilities and other disabled sports. It is a sister organisation to the British Olympic Association (BOA) serving as it does sport for the disabled as the BOA serves able-bodied sports in the U.K. **The aims** and objectives of the BPA include the organisation, funding and co-ordination of British teams competing in the Paralympic games and other approved international events. **It also maintains** close links with the BOA, the Sports Council and the Government through the Minister of Sport.

ACKNOWLEDGEMENTS

We would like to say a big thank you to all these people without whom we could not have produced this book. **A very special** thank you to David Abbott and Peter Mead from Abbott Mead Vickers BBDO and Sholto Douglas-Home from British Telecom whose last minute intervention saved this project from falling at the last hurdle. **Thank you** to Sara Lloyd and Chris Taylor at Ilford UK Ltd for providing us with the photographic materials and for being able to see the potential in the project after seeing only a handful of prints. Likewise, Ian Burrows from Sunrise Medical Ltd who has been with us from the beginning. Ruth Simmons for her energy, vitality and total belief in not only our photographs, but the Paralympic movement in general. Steve Gardiner and Debbie Downing from Steve Gardiner Design for all the late nights and for producing such a fabulous design in a short space of time. Jeremy Greenwood of Quiller Press for his patience and for standing by us. John Bailey for introducing us to the world of disabled sport. The British Paralympic Association, Matchtight Media, all the organisers from the different sporting disciplines, and all at Photographic Techniques. **To family**, friends and strangers at parties who have had to put up with us talking about it for the last two years. **But most of all**, to all the athletes who gave us a few minutes of their time and whose commitment, dedication, and achievements spurred us on. This book is of course for you.

Good luck.

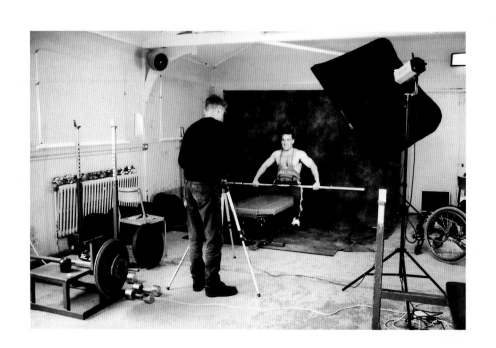